The Hudson Plane
Landing

Essential Events

THE HUDSON PLANE
LANDING
BY MARTIN GITLIN

Content Consultant
Terry L. von Thaden, PhD
University of Illinois at Urbana Champaign

ABDO
Publishing Company

CREDITS

Published by ABDO Publishing Company, PO Box 398166, Minneapolis, MN 55439. Copyright © 2012 by Abdo Consulting Group, Inc. International copyrights reserved in all countries. No part of this book may be reproduced in any form without written permission from the publisher. The Essential Library™ is a trademark and logo of ABDO Publishing Company.

Printed in the United States of America,
North Mankato, Minnesota
092011
012012

 THIS BOOK CONTAINS AT LEAST 10% RECYCLED MATERIALS.

Editor: Andrew Cleary
Copy Editor: Chelsea Whitcomb
Cover design: Marie Tupy
Interior design and production: Kazuko Collins

Library of Congress Cataloging-in-Publication Data
Gitlin, Marty.
  The Hudson plane landing / by Martin Gitlin.
      p. cm. -- (Essential events)
  Includes bibliographical references.
  ISBN 978-1-61783-309-0
  1. Airplanes--Ditching--Hudson River (N.Y. and N.J.) 2.
Airplane crash survival--Hudson River (N.Y. and N.J.) 3. US
Airways Flight 1549 Crash Landing, Hudson River, N.Y. and
N.J., 2009. 4. Aircraft accidents--Hudson River (N.Y. and N.J.)
5. Aircraft bird strikes--Hudson River (N.Y. and N.J.) I. Title.
  TL711.D5G58 2012
  363.12'4--dc23
                                            2011036127

TABLE OF CONTENTS

Captain Chesley Sullenberger, left, and First Officer Jeffrey Skiles go through an average preflight routine.

I read this book

JUST ANOTHER DAY?

rina Levshina is not superstitious. But an eerie feeling washed over her on January 15, 2009. The Russian immigrant was scheduled to fly that afternoon from New York City to Charlotte, North Carolina. She would then take another plane to meet her husband in Las Vegas, Nevada. Yet something was telling her to cancel the trip.

Though it was a strong intuition, Levshina believed there was no logical reason for such fear. She also thought her husband would be disappointed if she did not show up. So she boarded Flight 1549 at LaGuardia Airport.

Pam Seagle experienced a more powerful warning. Four nights earlier she had a terrifying nightmare of a plane crash. But she could not cancel her flight. She worked for Bank of America, which is based in Charlotte, and was returning home from a business trip.

Each of the 150 passengers that stepped onto the US Airways Airbus A320 that cold day had a different story. There was 85-year-old Lucille Palmer, who ignored a plea from her son not to fly because of the wintry weather. She wanted to visit Charlotte to celebrate her great-grandson's first birthday.

There was Jeff Kolodjay, one of six buddies on the flight from the tiny town of Chicopee, Massachusetts. He eagerly awaited a golfing trip with his friends and father in Myrtle Beach, South Carolina.

There was television executive Billy Campbell, whose network had produced the story of United Flight 93. That plane had been hijacked on September 11, 2001, and crashed after its heroic passengers fought back against the hijackers.

The passenger list on Flight 1549 included 95 men, 52 women, two young children, and a nine-month-old baby boy. Some had the same haunting feelings as Levshina and Seagle. Others were simply afraid of flying. But to most, it was just another flight on just another day.

Déjà vu?

Passengers on board the same Airbus taking an identical route two days earlier might have predicted problems. They heard a series of

---

A Tour of New York City

Many passengers were quiet as they settled in to their seats on Flight 1549. But Gerard P. McNamara was busy speaking with a young businessman seated next to him.

McNamara had flown the New York-to-Charlotte flight many times. He enjoyed looking at the sights below and pointed out several of them to his new friend as the flight gained speed and left the ground.

McNamara and his fellow passengers could see a number of famous landmarks from the plane as it soared toward the sky. There was the George Washington Bridge, which rises over the Hudson River to connect New Jersey to New York. There was the Bronx Zoo, which covers more than 200 acres (81 ha) of land in New York City and holds more than 600 species of animals from around the world. The passengers would also have been able to see Yankee Stadium in the Bronx, where major league baseball's New York Yankees play their home games.

banging noises in flight and were told by the crew that an emergency landing was possible. Passenger Steve Jeffrey recalled,

> It sounded like the wing was just snapping off. The red lights started going on. A little pandemonium was going on. It seemed so loud, like luggage was hitting the side but times a thousand. . . . It wasn't turbulence, it wasn't luggage bouncing around. It was just completely like the engine was thrown against the side of the plane.[1]

That flight continued and the pilot soon explained the noise. Jeffrey did not fully understand the explanation. "He made it sound like the air didn't get to the engine and it stalled the engine out," Jeffrey said.[2]

On the flight two days later, it would appear pilots Chesley "Sully" Sullenberger and Jeffrey Skiles could handle anything thrown their way. Fifty-seven-year-old Sullenberger was particularly experienced. He had been flying planes for 40 years and had worked with US Airways since 1980. He had logged 770 hours of flight time over the past year.

Fateful Introduction

Pilots Sullenberger and Skiles met for the first time only three days before they handled Flight 1549.

The two were paired for a four-day trip on different airplanes to various destinations. The flight from New York to Charlotte was the first for Sullenberger in two weeks.

There was nothing on that winter afternoon that led him to believe the trip would be more eventful than any other. Though Sullenberger, as captain, was in charge of the plane, it was First Officer Skiles's turn to do the primary flying. Sullenberger had faith in his partner, who was also a skilled and seasoned pilot.

As the pilots prepared to start the engines, a flight attendant gave her usual safety speech to the passengers. She stressed the importance of wearing their seat belts. She pointed out the emergency exits and told them their seat cushions could be used as flotation devices.

NOT REALLY LISTENING

Few were paying close attention to her words. They assumed, as airplane passengers generally do, that their flight would be safe. Some had begun nodding off for a nap they hoped would last until they landed.

The conditions outside were ideal for flying. It had snowed that

Birth of an Airport

LaGuardia Airport was named after the man responsible for making it a reality. Fiorello LaGuardia was mayor of New York City in the 1930s. He became upset one day when his flight landed in New Jersey because New York City had no airport, so he set the wheels in motion to have one built. LaGuardia Airport opened for business in 1939.

LaGuardia Airport is one of the busiest airports in the country.

morning, but now the sun was shining. Traffic on the runway was light. The air traffic controller had no trouble handling the inbound and outbound flights. At 3:21 p.m., he placed Flight 1549 at the departure end of Runway 4. The pilots waited for two other planes to land. Four minutes later, they were ready to take off.

Skiles flew the Airbus to 500 feet (152.40 m). He took a 20-degree left turn from northeast to north and began the initial ascent.

"Climbing to 5,000 [feet (1,524 m)]," Sullenberger reported to Departure Control, which was monitoring the flight.

"Cactus 1549," controller Patrick Harten replied. "New York departure, radio contact. Climb and maintain 15,000 [feet (4,572 m)]."[3]

Everything seemed fine. Sullenberger expressed delight at the pleasant turn of the weather and the view of the Hudson River. He retracted the flaps, which was necessary for the next stage of the ascent. The takeoff portion of the flight had been completed. Those passengers unafraid of flying were relaxed. Some had already fallen asleep.

The plane had been in the air for only a moment and had not yet reached 3,000 feet (914 m) when Sullenberger saw birds approaching.

Terror was about to take over Flight 1549.

The Hudson River flows down the west side of New York City,
past the tip of lower Manhattan.

*Chesley Sullenberger received part of his pilot's training
at the Air Force Academy.*

THE MOLDING OF A PILOT

ilots are little more than friendly voices to most airplane passengers. Passengers do not see pilots in the cockpit. Those who fly planes for a living do so with little recognition from the public.

People rarely consider the many hours of training required for pilots. Extensive training allowed Chesley Sullenberger to save the lives of his US Airways passengers on that fateful January afternoon.

Pilots are trained for emergencies. They do not simply spend their training time flying straight and level. After all, skill is not all that is tested when an emergency arises. Pilots must also stay cool under pressure with the lives of passengers at stake. The lessons Sullenberger learned in more than 40 years of piloting experience helped transform him into a national hero.

Sullenberger was born on January 23, 1951, and raised in Denison, Texas. His first desire as a young child was to be a firefighter or policeman. But by the age of five, he was already dreaming of a career as a pilot. He got a thrill watching jet fighters from the nearby Perrin Air Force Base zoom across the sky.

He wrote about the experience in his autobiography:

> Because it was such a rural area, the jets flew pretty low, at about 3,000 feet [914 m], and you could always hear them coming. My dad would give me his binoculars, and I loved looking into the distance, to the horizon, wondering what was

out there. It fed my [desire to become a pilot]. . . . What was out there was even more exciting because it was coming closer and closer at a very high rate of speed. . . . Every aspect of airplanes was fascinating — the different sounds they made, the way they looked, the physics that allowed them to rocket through the sky, and most of all, the men who controlled them with obvious mastery.[1]

A Horrible Day

September 11, 2001, began like a typical day for Sullenberger, but it was not going to be a typical day for any American.

Sullenberger was driving to San Francisco, California, to catch a plane to Pittsburgh, Pennsylvania. From there he would pilot a flight to Charlotte. Listening to the news on the radio, he heard that a plane had crashed into the North Tower of the World Trade Center in New York City.

He wondered how any pilot could fly that far off course. He assumed it was very foggy that morning. As he walked into the San Francisco airport, he heard that another plane had struck the South Tower and yet another hit the Pentagon in Washington DC. He and millions of other Americans then realized it was a terrorist attack.

Every plane flying above the United States was ordered to land. Approximately 35,000 flights were canceled. Sullenberger returned home to watch the news on television. He was horrified as the towers crashed to the ground and thousands of Americans were killed.

Sullenberger did not pilot a plane until three days later, but most Americans were not ready to fly again. He transported just seven passengers on that flight.

His First Plane Ride

Sullenberger began reading everything he could about flying. He recalls with joy his first plane trip at age 11. He describes as magical his feelings for Love Field, the Dallas airport from which he flew.

He was happy when his mother gave him a window seat on the plane. He pressed his face against the window and felt excited when the plane sped down the runway and took off. Everything below him looked small and insignificant compared to the majesty of the sky. He knew then for certain that he wanted to be a pilot.

Sullenberger began taking flying lessons at age 16. Though as a teenager he was shy, his instructor noted his enthusiasm. Sullenberger worked as a janitor in a church to help pay for his training. He took 16 lessons from a crop-dusting pilot; the lessons covered more than seven hours, and Sullenberger was soon flying solo. As he explained in his autobiography, it was an experience he still cherishes.

Sad Lesson

Sullenberger learned a harsh but valuable lesson as a teenage student pilot. One day his instructor showed him a wrecked plane with the blood of a dead pilot splattered in the cockpit. The plane had struck some power lines crossing along the highway and fallen to the ground.

Sullenberger realized from that moment that one mistake could result in the loss of life. Flying safely meant being aware of everything in the sky.

Charles Lindbergh was one of Sullenberger's childhood heroes. But Lindbergh gained fame 24 years before Sullenberger was born.

Lindbergh was the first pilot to fly solo across the Atlantic Ocean. He became a hero in the United States and beyond in 1927, when he flew his *Spirit of St. Louis* plane from New York to Paris, France.

Sullenberger built a model of that plane at age six. He later read all about the famed flight and marveled at how much planning and preparation it required.

"Climbing to 800 feet [244 m] above the ground, and then circling the field, I felt an exhilarating freedom," he writes. "I also felt a certain mastery. After listening, watching, asking questions, and studying hard, I had achieved something. Here I was, alone in the air."[2]

The cockpit became the most comfortable place in the world for Sullenberger. He was shy and studious. He took his flying seriously.

He learned more about his chosen profession after attending the US Air Force Academy in 1969. He was named Outstanding Cadet in Airmanship in 1973, reaching the rank of captain that same year. He remained in the Air Force throughout the decade. But cuts in the US military budget by the end of the 1970s helped convince him to become a commercial airline pilot.

As a cadet at the US Air Force Academy, Sullenberger learned to fly fighter planes.

A New Career

In 1980, Sullenberger landed a poorly paid job with Pacific Southwest Airlines, which was

Sullenberger does not see the same fascination with flying among children that he experienced in his youth, and that upsets him.

As a pilot, he would often see kids board his plane without even glancing at the cockpit. Instead, they would be busy playing their video games. That is why when children did show an interest, he would often allow them to look inside the cockpit. Sometimes he would let them sit down in his seat and take pictures. He would place a captain's hat on their heads and answer any questions they had about flying.

later bought by US Airways. He earned less than $200 a week. He soon discovered that his military background meant little to his future. Only seniority—time spent on one job—led to promotions in his new profession. He became a captain after eight years at Pacific Southwest.

Jeffrey Skiles also began flying as a teenager, and flew a variety of planes before joining Sullenberger as a pilot of the Airbus A320. Both of Skiles's parents were pilots, and Skiles spent some of his teenage years as a young pilot flying with his father over Alaska. Before becoming a passenger plane pilot, Skiles was a flight instructor and flew cargo planes. While he had only approximately 35 hours of flying time with an Airbus, he had logged years as a pilot and flight engineer of similar aircraft for US Airways.

Sullenberger loves to fly. He also feels he is doing a great service to the passengers and to the country, as he revealed in his autobiography:

> *It feels good to take a planeload of 183 people where they need or want to go. My job is to reunite people with family and friends, to send them on long-awaited vacations, to bring them to loved ones' funerals, to get them to their job interviews. . . . By the end of the day, after piloting three or four trips, I've taken four or five hundred people safely to their destinations, and I feel as if I've accomplished something. All of them have their own stories, motivations, needs—and helping them brings a rewarding feeling.*[3]

The airline industry struggled financially through the first decade of the twenty-first century. Pilots have lost flight time and have had their salaries significantly cut. After the Flight 1549 landing, Sullenberger expressed concern to the US Congress that poor wages will cause harm to the airline industry. He believes low pay results in young people shying away from becoming pilots.

"I am worried that the airline piloting profession will not be able to continue to attract the best and the brightest," he said.[4]

It became apparent on January 15, 2009, that Sullenberger and Skiles were among those best and brightest. It did not take just any flock of birds to bring that out. Bird strikes are fairly common. But a bird strike such as the one Sullenberger and Skiles encountered would test their skill as pilots, as well as their concentration and composure. ⌐

Many birds make their home in New York City, like these ducks seen floating near John F. Kennedy Airport.

Some airports use radar units to help detect birds before they can collide with aircraft.

WINGED, FLYING PESTS

The birth of flight dates back just over a century. So does the first confrontation between airplane and bird.

The deed was done by none other than Orville Wright, who had teamed with his brother Wilbur to launch the first powered flight in 1903. Five years later, Orville was flying over a cornfield near Dayton, Ohio, when he struck and killed a bird. The first human death in such a collision occurred in 1912.

Hundreds of thousands of bird strikes have since taken place throughout the country. The high total is not a surprise, considering the numbers of birds and planes in the sky. There are an average of 28,000 commercial airline flights per day in the United States and an estimated 6 billion birds in the country. They are all potential casualties.

Since the start of the twenty-first century, the National Wildlife Strike Database has recorded 98,700 bird strikes in the United States. Among the victims have been 370 different species of birds. Included are herons, storks, pelicans, swans, ducks, vultures, hawks, eagles, cranes, seagulls, pigeons, owls, turkeys, blackbirds, crows, and parrots.

Bird strikes can take place at any height. Some birds fly above 20,000 feet (6,096 m) in the air, and strikes have occurred as high as 32,000 feet (9,754 m). More than half of all birds hit by planes are struck within 100 feet (30 m) of the ground. Birds fly up when startled and often hit low-flying planes taking off or landing.

Canada geese flying around New York are particularly unsafe. There are large numbers of them and a huge number of flights leaving and entering the most populous city in the United States. In 1970, the estimated number of Canada geese in the United States was 200,000. According to the US Fish and Wildlife Service, that number had soared to 3.2 million in 2009.

An estimated 25,000 Canada geese make their homes in New York City. Approximately 20,000 more migrate through the area every year. Those that reside in that huge city generally stay within five miles (8 km) of their home. Many of them nest a short distance from LaGuardia Airport.

Getting Rid of Geese

Some concerned people have sought to reduce the Canada geese population by killing them off or

Not Just Birds

Planes that are departing or landing have hit ground animals as well as birds. Recorded hit victims have included rabbits, deer, moose, turtles, raccoons, porcupines, iguanas, snakes, skunks, chipmunks, and alligators. Even a wild pig and donkey have been struck by airplanes since the start of the twenty-first century.

removing them from the area. The organized killing of birds has been criticized by animal rights activists and others.

The Canada geese that were on a collision course with Flight 1549 were not New York residents. Scientists from the Feather Identification Laboratory determined they had migrated from Canada. Carla Dove, who serves as the laboratory's program director, explained why it is critical to understand that. "It is important to not only know what species of birds are involved

Controversial Culling

The collision with Flight 1549 resulted in the culling, or organized killing, of Canada geese near LaGuardia Airport. But that undertaking had been in practice in New York City for many years.

The largest number of nesting geese in New York assembled on Rikers Island, which rests near the departure end of Runway 4. That runway is where the ill-fated Airbus left the ground on January 15, 2009.

Geese have been targeted for culling by a number of government agencies, including the US Department of Agriculture. LaGuardia Airport employs wildlife management experts to spot and destroy Canada geese and their nests.

The culling effort was stepped up after the Flight 1549 incident. A plan to kill 2,000 birds in more than 40 parks in New York City was implemented. Animal activists groups, including one called the Coalition to Prevent the Destruction of Canada Geese, have criticized the culling. But city official Edward Skyler defended it. "Clearly, geese are a threat to aviation safety, and we can't count on miracles," he said. ". . . The intention is to do whatever we can to make the airspace around the airport safer."[1]

Others complained that the plan was a waste because it targeted just a small percentage of the resident and migrating Canada geese in the area.

Canada geese can be found on many beaches and waterfronts around New York City.

in collisions, but to also understand the role that migration plays in the larger picture," Dove said. "The more information we are able to gather in cases like this, the more we will be able to reduce the risks of bird strikes in the future."[2]

Birds had rarely been detected on the radar of air traffic controller Patrick Harten. When he had detected them, it was most often only because pilots confirmed their existence. The Canada geese that were apparent to the pilots of Flight 1549 did not appear on Harten's radar. Even if they had, he could not have warned Sullenberger and Skiles. There is no way to determine from radar the height of birds in the air.

The geese might not have heard the plane approaching. Though their hearing is similar to that of humans, they could have been deaf to the Airbus. The engines on that plane are designed to make a buzzing sound rather than a roar.

Researchers believe geese also boast far greater peripheral vision than humans. Rather than seeing straight ahead, they have a much

Addling to Subtract Geese

Some companies in New York and surrounding states are hired to get rid of unwanted geese. One method they use is "addling," which must be permitted by the federal government.

Addlers take eggs from goose nests and coat them with corn oil to prevent oxygen from reaching the embryo. Addlers might also shake the shells vigorously, destroying the embryos inside.

larger field of view. That might have prevented them from understanding they were on course to collide with the plane until it was too late.

University of Rhode Island zoology professor Dr. Frank Heppner suggested the birds were aware of the plane and its danger. He said it is possible they believed the plane would move out of their way.

Goose strikes are fairly uncommon. There were approximately 80 recorded goose strikes in the New York City area during the decade previous to the Flight 1549 collision. Strikes of other birds during that same period totaled approximately 4,000. But the size and wingspan of Canada geese make them more dangerous than most other birds.

Collision Course

When Sullenberger first noticed birds approaching his plane, he did not realize they were Canada geese. But soon they were everywhere in his sight, large in numbers and size.

A few of the passengers noticed something was wrong. Ricardo Valeriano stared out the window and thought he saw military aircraft ahead. Mark Hood said later he watched what he called "this gray blob just shoot by."[3]

A Delta Airlines plane shows the damage that can be done by a collision with a flock of large birds.

Skiles thought at first that the birds were going to fly under the plane. He was wrong. The Airbus was traveling north at 250 miles per hour (402 km/h). The birds were flying southwest at approximately 50 miles per hour (80 km/h), and they were headed for disaster.

Sullenberger stated the obvious in one word. "Birds!" he said. Skiles exclaimed, "Whoa!"[4]

It was too late to prevent the collision. Skiles and Sullenberger were about to receive the toughest test ever of their piloting skills and coolness under intense pressure. Their passengers and crew would soon receive the scare of their lives. ⌐

Some airports fire noisemaking shells into the air to scare away birds.

Pilots control a plane using a complex set of instruments and displays.

THE COLLISION

A t precisely 3:27 p.m. on January 15, 2009, five Canada geese struck Flight 1549. Two of them hit the left engine. Another slammed into the right engine. The collisions created a thumping noise that could be heard from the front of the plane to the back. A single voice expressed the shock and fear felt by all the passengers. It was a scream that came from 56-year-old department store merchandise manager Eileen Shleffar, who was a fearful flyer. She later admitted her embarrassment. After all, nobody else had shrieked like she had. But many of the others were simply stunned silent.

Not for long. Three other passengers later claimed they thought the plane had been hit by a terrorist attack. Stephen Lis, a 42-year-old executive from Philadelphia, thought the plane had been hit by a missile. Bank of America employee Warren Holland also feared the worst. "My first thought was a bomb in the cockpit or luggage compartment," he said. "I knew it was catastrophic."[1]

Some heard thuds as the birds struck the wings and other parts of the plane. To the passengers in the back rows, the collisions made a popping noise. To those closer to the strikes, it sounded more like a series of explosions. Accounting firm executive John Howell heard the thuds and saw several geese bouncing along the side of the plane. He vividly recalled the sight of one large goose with its body pointing forward and neck twisted back.

Raising a Stink

Many of the passengers saw dark objects getting sucked into the engines, but only some knew they were birds. The birds were killed instantly. The thud of the bird strike was followed by grinding noises inside the engines.

Television executive Billy Campbell saw a fire burst forth from the left engine soon after the birds hit. Amber Wells, who was returning to her North Carolina home, watched a fireball and black smoke coming from the right engine. The cabin filled with smoke and a burning smell.

Designed to Survive

Airplane engines are built to withstand bird strikes, but they are simply not capable of surviving the collisions such as those experienced by Flight 1549. In creating a set of rules for engine construction, the Federal Aviation Administration (FAA) cited three bird sizes: small, medium, and large.

The small birds weigh less than 3.3 ounces (93.6 g). Medium-sized birds, such as seagulls, are classified as weighing up to 2.5 pounds (1.1 kg). Because small birds most often fly in large and dense flocks, they are the most likely to cause multiple collisions with aircraft engines. Manufacturers must prove that their engines can handle at least 16 small birds and continue to provide thrust.

Engines have generally shown to be reliable in withstanding strikes from small and medium-sized birds. But engines have yet to be built that can reliably survive a strike with heavier birds. The regulations do not require that engines continue to provide thrust when hit by birds of that size. They only state that they must allow pilots to maintain control of their planes.

"It was putrid and instantaneous, burning flesh or fuel or whatever combination," said New Yorker Alex Magness. "It was unique, a terrible smell." Fellow passenger Ricardo Valeriano was also overwhelmed by the odor, calling it "a distinct smell of jet fuel, burning hair, and burning flesh. It's a concoction you never want to smell in your life, especially when you're in an airplane."[2]

Passenger Darren Beck, who was headed home to Charlotte, saw a sickening sight when he gazed into one of the engines. "The fan blades, that are normally, you know, perfectly aligned, were just mangled," he said. "It was shocking. It definitely left a sickening feeling in your stomach."[3]

The pilots could not allow themselves to be overtaken by fear. But Sullenberger was certainly stunned by the bird strike. He wrote later:

> As the birds hit the plane, it felt like we were being pelted by heavy rain or hail. It sounded like the worst thunderstorm I'd ever heard back in Texas. The birds struck many places on the aircraft below the level of the windshield, including the nose, wings, and engines. The thuds came in rapid succession, almost simultaneously but a fraction of a fraction of a second apart.[4]

He quickly noted that both engines had lost power. Jet engines suck in outside air and send it back at high speeds to propel planes forward and give them energy and speed. The simple workings of jet engines result in very few failures. But the engines on the Airbus that afternoon began winding down within three seconds after the birds hit.

GOING . . . GOING . . . GONE

The effect on the plane was immediate. The Airbus lost power and slowed dramatically. Skiles was still in control. The plane continued to rise as its nose remained pitched up slightly. Sullenberger attempted in vain to restore power.

He attempted to fire up the engines by starting the ignition. They did not respond. They were simply not designed to withstand a collision with large geese. They were built at a time when regulations demanded they withstand a strike with a bird that weighs up to four pounds (1.8 kg). The Airbus collided with multiple Canada geese, all of which together weighed at least three times that.

Sullenberger had never flown a plane that had experienced an engine failure. He was now in charge of one that had lost power in both engines. As soon

LaGuardia Airport is placed in the middle of New York City's dense neighborhoods and highways.

as he understood that both engines had been affected, he took over control of the plane from Skiles. As captain of the flight, it was Sullenberger's duty to take full control of the plane's descent.

The pilots made no immediate comment to their passengers. Following their training, they were sizing up the situation. They knew that bird strikes could be deadly. An estimated 229 passengers have been killed by bird strikes or rare runway collisions with land animals in the last 30 years. Nearly 200 planes have been destroyed in such incidents.

Sullenberger had been piloting for more than 40 years and had experienced a few bird strikes. None had even dented his plane. But he understood that every one of the 155 people on Flight 1549, which included himself and his crew, was in grave danger. They were only 3,000 feet (914 m) over New York City. They were pointed away from LaGuardia Airport. They were destined to descend with virtually no power in their engines.

The passengers quickly realized the danger as well. Some of them feared they were all doomed, but nobody panicked yet. Charlotte software salesman Jay McDonald recalled his feelings clearly. "I'm frozen in my seat, looking ahead, listening to people, and conversations are going on everywhere, slightly louder than normal," he said. "Nobody seemed hysterical. It was just a lot of rhetorical questions to the world: What's happening? Are we going to blow up? Are we going to crash? Why isn't the captain telling us?"[5]

Sullenberger was too busy trying to save 155 lives. There was not a second to lose. ⌐

Seconds after colliding with Canada geese, Flight 1549 descended over the Hudson River.

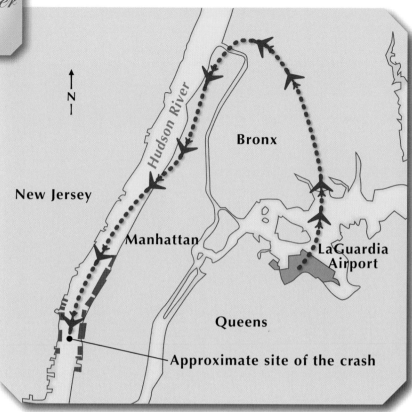

Sullenberger and Skiles's flight path over New York City
left little room for error.

CALM ON THE OUTSIDE,
PANIC ON THE INSIDE

ear became the dominant emotion for
the passengers and crew on Flight 1549.
Minds began racing from the moment they realized
the engines had lost their thrust and the plane was
going down.

Among those who later expressed their terror was 24-year-old passenger Michele Davis. She was afraid her family in Olympia, Washington, would never again see her alive. She wrote later:

I was so scared. I was running thoughts in my head. This can't be happening to me. They say that your past flashes before you, but it was my future that was flashing before me; the future I thought I wouldn't have. I want to see my niece grow up. . . . I want to have babies, see my mom, marry a good man. I want to see my grandma! . . . This can't be it![1]

Many were convinced it *was* the end. Some began praying quietly. Others took out their cell phones, but most were too frozen in fear to call loved ones. Still others attempted to calm their fellow passengers while overcoming their own feelings of panic.

Forty-four-year-old frequent flyer Jim Whitaker and young mother Tess Sosa shared a tense conversation. As Sosa cradled her ninth-month-old son in her arms, she turned to Whitaker.

"What's happening?" she asked. "Are we going to be okay?"

"Oh, an engine problem," he replied. "I've had this happen before. No worries."

"How do you know?" Sosa asked.

"I just know," reassured Whitaker.

Whitaker did not know. He, too, feared for his life. He was just trying to keep Sosa calm. "I was pathologically lying the whole time," he later admitted.[2]

Strange Time for a Phone Call?

Jay McDonald could not believe his eyes when he saw a fellow passenger talking on her cell phone after the bird strike on Flight 1549. He wondered why anyone would want a loved one to know the danger she was in.

That passenger was Eileen Shleffar, who admitted she is addicted to talking on the phone. She called her husband, David, and began an unusual conversation. She failed to express to him at first what was happening.

"What's going on now?" he asked. "Are you OK?"

"I don't know what's going on," she answered. "Something is burning badly."

"Are you at the airport?" he asked.

"Oh my god, it's so quiet in here," she said.

"What do you mean?" he asked. "Are you at the airport?"

David had no idea what she was talking about. When she finally expressed to him the danger she was in, he became alarmed.

"As it turns out, he was at the car wash," Shleffar explained later. "He said to the attendants, 'Get out, get out!' He threw the tip money at them and jumped in his car and took off. He drove home like a madman."[3]

A Man Who Could Not Panic

Sullenberger could not let his distress affect his concentration. The lives of 154 others were in his hands. He had to remain calm enough to allow his years of training and experience help fly the plane down safely.

Sullenberger felt confident, after taking over the controls

from Skiles, that he was the right man for the job. Both Skiles and Sullenberger had tens of thousands of hours of flight experience, but Sullenberger had more experience flying the Airbus A320. Meanwhile, Sullenberger trusted Skiles to find the right emergency procedures in a long list from the Quick Reference Handbook and carry them out. Skiles could use his experience to run the plane through system checks and shutdown lists, allowing Sullenberger to focus on guiding the plane and finding a place to land it.

Though he could hardly believe such a disaster had occurred, Sullenberger gained tremendous focus on the challenges ahead. As he later wrote:

> I was able to force myself to set those thoughts aside almost instantly. Given the gravity of the situation, I knew that I had seconds to decide on a plan and

Different Passengers, Different Prayers

A number of religions and nationalities were represented among the 150 passengers on Flight 1549. There were Christians, Jews, one Hindu, and one Muslim. As terror gripped the passengers, those differences did not matter.

One example was the exchange between Tracey Wolsko, Vicki Barnhardt of North Carolina, and Russian immigrant Irina Levshina. Wolsko helped calm the other two. Then the three of them held hands and prayed. Wolsko and Barnhardt spoke in English. Levshina prayed silently in Russian.

minutes to execute it. I was aware of my body. I could feel an adrenaline rush. I'm sure that my blood pressure and pulse spiked. But I also knew I had to concentrate on the tasks at hand and not let the sensations in my body distract me.[4]

Sullenberger quickly acknowledged to Skiles that thrust had been lost from both engines. Air traffic controller Harten was unaware of their situation. The plane still looked normal on his radar screen. He was soon to learn the truth.

"Mayday, Mayday, Mayday," Sullenberger called to him. " . . . Hit birds. We lost thrust in both engines. We're turning back towards LaGuardia."[5]

Harten kept his composure. He never hesitated. He knew time was of the essence. He told Sullenberger to turn his plane 220 degrees southwest.

Handling Something New

The loss of both engines was not just a new experience for Sullenberger. The same was true for air traffic controller Patrick Harten.

Sullenberger had faith in Harten, who had come through in previous emergencies. On one occasion, a plane entering LaGuardia Airport from overseas had enough fuel for 30 more minutes of flight. Due to bad weather, the plane was in a holding pattern. Harten ordered another aircraft to delay its arrival so the plane that was low on fuel could land. The maneuvering was executed perfectly.

From Plane to Glider

Sullenberger gained confidence knowing that modern planes were designed to glide through the air over long distances. He glided the plane with the landing gear and flaps up. He lowered its nose to achieve the most efficient gliding speed. These adjustments would help him glide the plane as far as it could go without engines. The smoothness of the descent from 2,900 feet (884 m) helped the passengers remain calm—as calm as can be under such dire circumstances.

What struck many passengers was that the plane was no longer making a sound as it drifted through the air. "There was just an absolute eerie silence from the plane like you've never heard," said Alex Magness. "You could have heard a pin drop."[6]

Harten ordered that all traffic to and from LaGuardia be stopped. Several airport landing options

Experience That Did Not Help

Sullenberger piloted gliders as a cadet in the Air Force Academy and taught the art of gliding in later years. One might assume such experience was helpful to him when both engines lost their power on Flight 1549.

Sullenberger said he did not believe that experience was useful during the emergency. He explained that the speed and weight of an Airbus are vastly different than those of a glider.

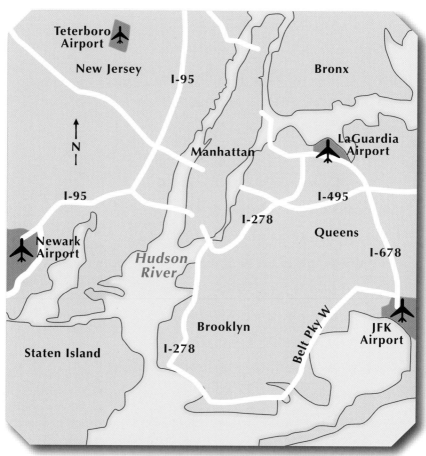

Sullenberger and Skiles were close to a number of airports in the New York City area.

remained for Flight 1549, but each of them could have resulted in the deaths of everyone on board, as well as possibly other innocent people. Harten hoped Sullenberger could land at LaGuardia or Teterboro Airport in nearby New Jersey.

LaGuardia features two 7,000-foot (2,134-m) runways. Sullenberger could have attempted to land on either one in either direction. He could have returned to Runway 4, which Flight 1549 had used to take off. But that runway is surrounded by a busy highway and a residential neighborhood. If the plane fell short of its target, the passengers and others could be killed.

Sullenberger quickly sized up the situation. The plane was not plummeting downward. He toyed with the idea of landing at Teterboro. But, as the plane descended under 2,000 feet (610 m), he realized that the best hope for survival was to land on the Hudson River. Many of the passengers also believed a splash landing was inevitable—and they were scared. Martin Sosa described the experience:

From War Zone to Flight 1549

Passenger Andrew Gray had experienced frightening moments before the Canada geese struck the engines of his plane. He had served two tours of duty with the US Army in the war in Afghanistan.

He sat alongside his fiancée Stephanie King, who could not stop crying. He had led 41 soldiers into a war zone, but felt helpless because he could not comfort his bride to be. "I just took her by the hand and kissed her and said, 'I love you,'" he recalled.[7]

My two biggest fears in life have been falling out of the sky or drowning. . . . I said to myself it doesn't look like we are going to the airport. I realized then that we were going into the water. . . . I was angry. I was cursing. A lot of people went into prayer. I was [swearing].

I was just angry. You couldn't believe this is happening to you. This was like the end of your life. You're going to just die. How is this going to play out? Is the plane going to disintegrate?[8]

The 150 passengers were about to find out.

*Harten and Sullenberger shook hands as they met on Capitol Hill
a month after the Hudson plane landing.*

Sullenberger returned to the cockpit months after the emergency landing of Flight 1549.

"Brace for Impact!"

Sullenberger had been flying planes for 42 years. When his instincts told him something as he sat in the cockpit, he listened. It was less than a minute after a bird strike had rendered the aircraft's engines all but useless, and his instincts told him he was not going to land Flight 1549 undamaged on a runway.

He understood that the plane was flying too low, too slow, and too distant from an airport to land there. He ruled out landing on a highway or residential neighborhood. Why risk killing citizens below in what could be a failed attempt to save passengers? If he tried to reach LaGuardia and fell short by even a few feet, the plane would likely rip open and burst into flames.

Sullenberger remained mentally organized and tried to stay calm. But it was not easy. "It was the worst, sickening, pit-of-your-stomach, falling through the floor feeling I've ever felt in my life," he said later.[1]

He realized that a rescue effort would be required no matter where the plane touched down. The rescue boats and other services on the Hudson River could reach the boat quickly. Rescue personnel at LaGuardia would take longer to arrive on the scene.

All those thoughts entered his mind in mere seconds and dictated his decision to land on the Hudson. But Sullenberger knew achieving such a landing was far more difficult than deciding to attempt it.

Harten tried to steer Sullenberger to LaGuardia, but Sullenberger told Harten firmly that it was impossible.

Sullenberger considered Teterboro Airport in New Jersey. A runway there was open. But just as Harten was preparing to direct the Airbus there, Sullenberger determined it was too far.

FATEFUL CONVERSATION

"You can land Runway One at Teterboro," Harten offered.

"We can't do it," Sullenberger replied.

"OK, which runway would you like at Teterboro?" Harten asked.

"We're gonna be in the Hudson," Sullenberger answered.[2]

Harten later told Congress he thought the

Flying to Flushing?

Sullenberger did have another option to land his plane in the water aside from the Hudson River. If he had decided to attempt to reach LaGuardia Airport and fallen short, he could have set the plane down in Flushing Bay.

Flushing Bay is a part of the East River, and it sits between the borough of Queens and the Bronx in New York City. LaGuardia Airport sits on the Queens shore of the bay, where it was built on landfill reclaimed from the bay's water.

Sullenberger decided against landing there. The bay was close to the airport, but Sullenberger knew that only a few outboard motorboats would be available there to rescue passengers. They would have to take too many trips to retrieve all 155 people on board of Flight 1549. In the meantime, many of the passengers could have drowned.

passengers were doomed. Many of the passengers felt the same way as the river drew closer in their sights. Charlotte patio door salesman Brad Wentzell believed at first the plane would strike the George Washington Bridge. When it cleared the bridge by just a few hundred feet, he knew there would be no airport landing and that the plane was destined for the Hudson.

Wentzell was one of many passengers who spoke about his or her conception of God. "There was no way [to reach LaGuardia]," he said. "I could feel us floating. . . . I said, 'Lord, I have not lived a perfect life. Please forgive me for my sins. Take care of my wife and daughter. Take me to the Gates of Heaven.'"[3]

Other passengers began thinking about death. Among them was 40-year-old Warren Holland. He was heading home to Charlotte and losing hope that he would return. Holland, a religious man, prayed. He later said,

> In the midst of that utter hopelessness, I was looking forward, as crazy as that may sound, to finding out about death. What's death going to be like? Complete darkness, bright light, perfect clarity, joy, salvation? What's it going to be like

On its descent toward the Hudson, Flight 1549 barely cleared the George Washington Bridge.

in the presence of God? I'm nothing special, but God gives us all hope in the direst of moments, that sense of hope and salvation.[4]

One man who did not believe he was about to die was Sullenberger. He had faith in Skiles's skills as first officer and in his plane. He was confident his three flight attendants would get the passengers safely out the exit doors after the plane hit water. He finally spoke seven words that both alerted and haunted the 150 passengers. They were the first words he uttered to them since the bird strike. "This is the captain," he announced. "Brace for impact!"[5]

The flight attendants sprang into action. They walked briskly through the cabin and spoke words the passengers would never forget. "Brace! Brace! Heads down! Stay down!" they repeated.[6]

"Emotional Chaos"

Jim Whitaker explained how his fellow passengers reacted to those commands:

> It was the trigger moment that released the emotional chaos inside the plane. Adrenaline and fear went into overdrive. People were crying, yelling, praying, holding hands, Ohmygods. The takeaway moment for me is looking at people near me and seeing that . . . genuine fear for one's life in their eyes.[7]

Whitaker did what he could to relieve that fear. He asked fellow

One Scare after Another

Passenger Barry Leonard had experienced one near tragedy and was facing another. Ten years earlier, his son was almost killed after getting smacked in the head with a baseball. Leonard was told his son could die on the way to the hospital. "That was the worst thing that happened to me in my life, not this," Leonard said in comparing the two events.[8]

Leonard was going through another family crisis in early 2009. His wife had been tested for breast cancer and was awaiting the results. As the plane dropped toward the Hudson River, Leonard prayed that God take his life instead of his wife's.

passenger Tess Sosa if he could hold her baby for her. He felt a strong man such as himself could better brace the child for the impending impact. He cradled the baby boy on his chest and braced himself against the seat in front of him.

In the cockpit, the automated voice on the Enhanced Ground Proximity Warning System repeated an alert Sullenberger was forced to ignore. It urged him to pull the plane up because it was about to strike the ground.

Different Kind of Danger

Chris Rini assumed that if he was going to die in a crash, it would be in a car. The Flight 1549 passenger is one of the top drag racers in the world.

Rini has driven his powerful Dodge Strata race car at speeds up to 200 miles per hour (322 km/h)—nearly as fast as the Airbus was traveling as it glided down toward the Hudson River.

The only control he had over the plane was to raise or lower its nose. He worked to maintain proper glide speed. If he felt the plane was coming in too fast, he raised the nose. If it slowed too much, he lowered it. He attempted to keep the wings level to avoid flipping the plane when it hit the water. Beside him, Skiles was working furiously to prepare the plane for a water landing.

It was only three minutes after the bird strike and the Airbus was about to slam into the Hudson River. The nightmare was far from over.

*Pilots use an Airbus A320 simulator to prepare
for the task of piloting the plane.*

Ferryboats were ready to surround the plane after it landed in the river.

THE CRASH

Many quiet prayers were spoken in the Airbus cabin as it dropped toward the Hudson River. Those solemn words were drowned out by the continued urging of the flight attendants. Their repeated orders for the passengers to brace and keep their heads down came faster and louder than before.

The pleas were annoying passenger Josh Peltz, so he gazed out the window and began a countdown that estimated the distance from the plane to the river: "Fifty feet . . . 40 feet . . . 35 feet . . . " Now Peltz was annoying a woman six rows back, who yelled, "Please stop! You're terrifying all of us."[1]

Passenger Steve O'Brien thought it was ironic that he was going to die on the Hudson River, where three of his grandparents had arrived in New York from Ireland many years ago. Brad Wentzell feared he would never see his three-year-old daughter again. Dan Vinton wondered if he was destined for heaven or would simply turn to dust.

Others took a more practical view. Jay McDonald assumed the plane would break apart upon landing and would be filled with water, so he hoped he could escape from a crack in the plane. Tracey Wolsko set her mind on survival and focused on using the exits. March Dolphin made it a point to not panic. She figured that calmness would be required by as many passengers as possible for them to survive.

What appeared to be an impending disaster had many outside witnesses. Nearby New Yorkers and

New Jersey residents peered out their windows to watch the Airbus drop toward the river. Sullenberger had managed to slow it down to 150 miles an hour (241 km/h). But the plane was traveling 13.5 feet per second (4.1 m/sec), three times faster than during a normal landing.

Impact!

The hard fall caused the belly of the Airbus to rip open when it struck the river at 3:31 pm. Onrushing icy water shredded the structure and ruptured the back wall of the plane.

The lower baggage area was crushed upward. A jagged beam crashed through the cabin floor next to flight attendant Doreen Welsh. The left engine ripped free and the plane slid forward in a wave of water spray. The Airbus skidded left, tipped to the right, and then stopped.

Soon the plane was floating. Sullenberger and Skiles turned to look at each other and said the exact same words at nearly the same time. "That wasn't as bad as I thought," they exclaimed.[2]

Watching the Drama Unfold

Many New York and New Jersey residents watched the Airbus drop into the Hudson River. Among them was basketball star Vince Carter, who was playing at that time for the New Jersey Nets.

Carter stared at the scene from the window of his condo as the jet passed by, gliding just above the water. He later told the *New York Daily News* that the experience was just like watching television.

A security camera at the Manhattan Cruise Terminal captured the landing of Flight 1549 in the Hudson River.

Passenger Raymond Mandrell later described the experience of the impact. "You ever been through any hurricanes?" he asked. "I know we were going hundreds of miles per hour. All the windows shattered, all you felt was air coming through the windows. You saw a bunch of ice coming through the windows. . . . [It was like] the whole plane was going to break apart into pieces."[3]

The pilots knew the plane would soon begin sinking. The cabin had 26 rows of seats with four main exit doors—two each in the front and back. The plane also had two emergency exits over each wing. The main exit doors were equipped with inflatable slides capable of detaching and could be used as rafts.

The passengers appeared too stunned to react for a few moments after the plane struck water. Some remained frozen in their seats. A few reached into the overhead bins for their luggage and other valuables,

---

Right Man for the Job

Many believe Sullenberger was the perfect pilot for Flight 1549. Among them is William Langewiesche, who wrote a book about the event, titled *Fly By Wire*. Langewiesche wrote:

[Sullenberger] was capable of intense mental focus and exceptional self-control. Normally these traits do not much matter for airline pilots, because teamwork and cockpit routines serve well enough. But [in landing the plane he] ruthlessly shed distractions, including his own fear of death. He had pared down his task to making the right decision about where to land, and had followed through with a high-stakes flying job. His performance was a work of extraordinary concentration.[4]

Author and former fighter pilot Don Sheppard marveled at Sullenberger's performance in the cockpit:

It's very important in a water landing to fly the aircraft onto the water as slow as possible. The faster you hit, the more likely the plane will cartwheel or the fuselage will disintegrate. Once the decision was made to [land in the water], it was a magnificent piece of aviation professionalism.[5]

which angered Wentzell. The time it took for that effort, he screamed, could cause people to drown.

GETTING OUT FAST

Sullenberger understood the importance of getting the passengers out as quickly and orderly as possible. He opened the cockpit door and ordered them to evacuate. Soon the aisle was jammed with frantic passengers trying to escape as the ice water rose up, particularly in the back. A few elbowed their way past others. Some jumped over seats in an attempt to reach the exits faster.

Eighty-five-year-old Lucille Palmer, who could hardly walk in ideal conditions, told her daughter, Diane Higgins, to leave her. That would have been suicide—the horrified Higgins would not hear of it. Denise Lockie, who remained hunched over in her seat, asked fellow passenger Mark Hood if they were in heaven. Hood exclaimed that he was no angel and urged her to get out. Barry Leonard had the same eerie feeling. He got up and then checked his seat to see if his body was still there.

The passengers near the front were lucky. They simply scurried to the first-class exit doors and into the rafts. Those in the middle of the plane evacuated quickly out the emergency wing exits. Michelle DePonte, Michael Whitesides, and Adelaide Horton had their left side exits open within approximately 15 seconds, allowing the passengers to escape.

The scene in the back of the plane, however, was one of terror and confusion. Icy water rushed in from the floorboards. It rose quickly to the waists of the passengers. Laurel Hubbard wondered how long it would take to drown. Her panic was justified—she cannot swim.

Many passengers did not realize the rear exits were under water and unusable. They rushed to the back of the plane. Flight attendant Doreen Welsh was frightened. The freezing water had reached her chest. Panicking passengers going in the wrong direction were racing toward her, and they were blocking the path to working exits.

"Go the other way!" she screamed.[6] Confusion reigned. Now the mass of people was not moving in either direction.

The passengers in the back were in trouble. And even those who had scrambled out of the plane were still not safe.

Rescue crews had to work fast to remove passengers before the plane sank in the river.

Rescue boats quickly gathered around the downed plane.

TRYING TO STAY ALIVE

*N*ews about the Airbus falling into the Hudson River quickly spread around New York and New Jersey. More important for the 155 on board, rescue personnel had been informed and were on their way.

The nearest was a commuter ferry called the *Thomas Jefferson*. That boat would require four minutes to reach the scene. With the plane slowly sinking, many who had evacuated feared they would be drowned by then.

The first passengers to reach the wings did not stay. Michelle DePonte ran to the end of the wing and leaped into the near-freezing water. Michael Whitesides followed. Soon several others had jumped into the river. None realized that the water was too cold and the distance to both the New Jersey and New York shores were too far to swim to safety.

"You had to explode out of that plane," explained Steve O'Brien. "The passengers were screaming 'Go! Go! Go!' You had to get out. It didn't occur to me to go onto the wing. At that point, nobody was on the wing."[1] O'Brien felt safe floating on his seat cushion in the water. While others

Get Those Life Vests!

Skiles noticed that some passengers had no life vests after the water landing. Many walked from the plane's cabin onto the wing with their seat cushions because they could not find the vests, which were underneath the seats. Skiles and Sullenberger quickly helped hand out life vests, as well as jackets and blankets, to shivering passengers on the wings.

believed they were still in grave danger, he knew he was destined to see his children again.

Some of the passengers said they smelled fuel pouring from the engine. They feared the Airbus would explode, and they yearned to get as far away from it as possible. Others thought they would be forced to jump in the water to avoid drowning on a sinking plane. But those on the left side of the first-class cabin jumped in because the life raft there failed to deploy. That caused many to race to the raft on the right side, which was still available.

Among those who jumped in the water was Barry Leonard. The icy Hudson caused him to hyperventilate. His breathing became so rapid that he found it difficult to swim. Leonard was experiencing what is known as cold-shock response, which can cause death. He managed to swim around the nose of the plane to the right-side raft.

Pam Seagle could understand what Leonard felt. She looked as if she had nearly frozen to death after trying to swim. Mark Hood, who pulled Seagle into the raft, said the icy water had taken a clear toll: "Pam looked to me like she was almost dead because her lips were so blue and her skin was so pale."[2]

FIRST ON THE WING

At the wing exit, Clay Presley watched others leap into the water in front of him. He figured they were all in the process of freezing to death. Because he did not have a seat cushion with him, he stepped with caution onto the wing. Jorge Morgado did the same and urged others not to jump in the water. It was a fateful moment. Those who had been swimming realized they had no chance to reach safety. Helping hands pulled them onto the wings.

Those outside were the lucky ones. The passengers in the back of the plane grew more frightened, panicked, and wet. The unusable back exit caused a mass of humanity to form as passengers ran into each other in search of escape. Meanwhile, the

Clear Thinking in a Disaster?

In the confusion following the landing, many passengers on Flight 1549 failed to heed the instructions the flight attendants had given in their preflight safety presentation. They did not grab their life vests or their seat cushions when the plane hit the water. These devices could have helped them float in the water as they waited to be rescued.

But Amanda Ripley, author of *The Unthinkable: Who Survives When Disaster Strikes*, understands. She says,

All the instructions they tell you to do—taking the life vests from your seat, grabbing a cushion as a flotation device— are all very difficult to follow in that kind of landing. Hitting the water is incredibly jarring. . . . The plane sinks quickly. You have to recover from the shock, unbuckle your seat belt and get out of the cabin. There is very little time to react.[3]

Passengers waited on the wings for rescue personnel.

water continued rising. *Miracle on the Hudson* authors William Prochnau and Laura Parker describe the commotion:

> It was a terrifying scene and it touched everyone in at least the last [six] rows, adding a grim dimension to the experience that separated them in a major way from the other survivors. Would they miraculously survive the crash only to suffer a ghastly death by drowning? There were frightening problems still ahead on the water outside, but standing in the back of a sinking airplane was a hideous prospect.[4]

Airbus Heroes

The panic did not prevent some from helping those who could not help themselves. Brad Wentzell embraced the role of hero by helping Tess Sosa and her baby evacuate from one of the wing exits. Wentzell later described the scene:

> *The water is waist deep, the aisle is blocked, and [Sosa] is trying to climb over the seats holding her baby and she's . . . sort of trapped. They both look scared to death. I say to myself, 'If you don't go back and help her, you'll never forgive yourself.' So I push one guy out of the way, and I get to them, and I just bear-hug her and the baby and say, 'Come on, you're coming with me.'[5]*

Putting Passengers to the Test

British researcher Helen Muir is among the world's foremost experts in passenger behavior. She ran a series of test evacuations that assessed the reaction of passengers in certain situations.

In one test, she offered money to the first 50 percent of passengers to evacuate a plane. Muir filmed the results. The same people who had been well behaved in previous tests raced up the aisles, pushed others out of the way, and climbed over seats. Muir's coworkers were forced to save people from being trampled and crushed.

Not everyone who remained on the plane was in a giving spirit. Alex Magness and March Dolphin both had flotation devices snatched from their hands by desperate passengers. But Vic Warnement later said that for every passenger who panicked, two others were there to bring calm.

Speedy Evacuation

Despite the frightening problems in the rear of the Airbus, the evacuation of Flight 1549 was completed quickly. Sullenberger expressed pride at the fact that the last passenger left the plane approximately three and a half minutes after the evacuation began.

Sullenberger walked down the aisle twice and shouted for anyone remaining on the plane to come forward. He was happy that nobody was left.

The passengers in the back eventually moved slowly in unison toward the wing exits, where they were escorted out by flight attendant Donna Dent. The last person to leave the back of the plane was Jim Hanks, a lawyer from Baltimore. He was certain he was about to die. He later described his thoughts at that moment:

> *This is it. I'm going to drown. My wife, Sabine, is going to be a young widow. My daughter, Maria Dorothy, is going to grow up without a father, and she's only four years old. She's not even going to remember me.*[6]

Hanks's fears were understandable, but needless. The plane was sinking tail first rather than evenly. As he moved forward, the water lowered from his shoulders, to his chest, and then to his waist. He escaped the cabin from the first-class exit and slid down the chute into the raft. The evacuation was complete. But 155 shivering people still needed to be rescued.

The Hudson River filled with rescue boats and personnel.

Some passengers left the plane in inflatable rafts.

THE RESCUE

he descent of Flight 1549 toward the Hudson River was witnessed only by those who were close enough to the scene in New York and New Jersey. The plight of the traumatized passengers and crew was seen by millions more as local and national television networks began airing the rescue. It was "reality TV" at its most dramatic. Viewers watched as 155 freezing people impatiently waited while boats and a police helicopter rushed to the scene. Only 33 of them wore life vests. Some passengers waited on off-wing slides while others stood perilously on wings or in rafts.

Captain Vincent Lombardi and his ferry, the *Thomas Jefferson*, were the first rescuers to arrive. They showed up just three minutes and fifty-five seconds after the plane came to a halt in the river. Lombardi felt duty-bound to help. "It's like an oath you take as a captain when you get your license, to assist others in peril at sea, in a river, anywhere in the water," he said.[1]

Other rescue boats had already arrived by the time Sullenberger emerged from the plane onto the left-side raft. He was encouraged that nobody was crying or shouting. They were mostly silent, perhaps because they were in shock from the harrowing experience.

The cold, felt particularly by those who had been drenched by water, was numbing. Passenger Larry Snodgrass claimed that if offered the choice between a million dollars and a dry pair of socks, he would have taken the socks. Jennifer Doyle exclaimed that her hands burned so badly from the cold they felt as though they were on fire.

Bill Zuhowski may have felt the cold more intensely than most. When the flight landed in the river, he was in the plane as it began to fill with water. Zuhowski felt weighed down by his shoes and clothes. So despite the icy water stinging his body, he removed his pants, shirt, and shoes. Then he grabbed a seat cushion and climbed over every seat until he reached the front exit. Soon Zuhowski was in a raft, waiting for rescue while stripped down to his boxer shorts.

Cutting the Cord

Though they had not been killed on contact with the river, the passengers on the raft had one last concern for their lives. The rafts remained tied to the plane. The nylon cord that tethered the rafts to the aircraft helped keep the rafts close as passengers exited the plane. But now the rafts could be pulled under by the sinking plane. None of the passengers or crew members had a knife to cut the cord. A knife was stored on each raft, but even Sullenberger did not know where.

Jeff Kolodjay attempted to chew through the cord, but not for long. He stopped when he tasted fuel.

Soon the deckhands on the *Thomas Jefferson* ferryboat came to the rescue. An elderly man pulled out a knife that passenger Douglas Schrift estimated to be six to eight inches (15 to 20 cm) long and tossed it. It sailed over Schrift's head to another passenger, who cut the cord. The knife was then tossed into the river to prevent it from puncturing the raft.

HELP ON THE WAY

Sullenberger was relieved and impressed by the number of boats floating to the sinking Airbus from both sides of the river. Many of the boat captains had received no order to come to the rescue but did so spontaneously. By the time the plane glided over the George Washington Bridge, hundreds of police officers, firefighters, and medics were converging on the Hudson. Within 30 minutes, more than 1,200 people were on the scene. New York is one of the few cities in the world that could mobilize so much help that quickly, as Sullenberger explained later:

> It was [fortunate] that we landed in the river right around Forty-eighth Street, just as several high-speed catamaran ferries were preparing for the afternoon rush hour. Across the river in New Jersey, at the . . . Ferry Terminal, the boats' captains and deckhands were

Worried Wife

Lorrie Sullenberger was not watching TV on the afternoon of January 15, 2009. She was not aware that her husband, Chesley, had saved 155 lives by landing a plane in the river.

Chesley Sullenberger called her from a ferry after the incident. He did not go into detail about the crash landing. He informed her that he had been forced to bring his plane down in the Hudson due to a bird strike and that he was safe. She lay on the bed and shook badly.

shocked to see our plane splash into the water. They were riveted by the sight of passengers almost immediately escaping from the plane. And in that instant, without being contacted by authorities and on their own initiative, they quickly headed our way.[2]

The passengers waiting on rafts waved the *Thomas Jefferson* and *Moira Smith*, the second vessel to arrive, to those stranded on the wings. They understood that the "wing walkers" were in greater danger. Though it appeared from a distance that the passengers stranded on the wings were calm, most were not. The wings were slippery and packed with people. Several had slipped into the river. One wing had already sunk a bit into the water.

New York Police Department Scuba Team detectives Michael Delaney and Robert Rodriguez aided the efforts along with the crews from

Humor on the Hudson

Some passengers used humor to help survive emotionally as they awaited rescue following the plane crash. Others joked because they were thrilled to be alive. A few passengers jokingly wondered how many frequent-flyer miles they had earned on the flight.

Crews of many boats assisted in the rescue operation.

14 boats. Upon seeing so many boats on the scene, Delaney first thought he would not be needed. He noticed the tail of the plane in the water and assumed there were dead passengers inside. Focusing on those who had exited the plane, Delaney helped a female passenger swim to a ferryboat with a ladder down to the water.

Soon all were working in harmony. Commuters on the ferries tossed life vests to shivering Airbus passengers. Firefighters lifted crash survivors to safety on their inflatable rafts. The Coast Guard worked to transfer people from the wings to the boats.

Thanks to the Captain

In the life raft, Skiles turned to Sullenberger to give him praise. It would be the kind of compliment to which Sullenberger would become accustomed. "You know, Sully, no one's ever done a successful ditch and you just pulled it off," Skiles said. "Pretty amazing."[3] Sullenberger replied that he thought it was going to be a lot worse.

So did air traffic controller Harten. He knew nothing about the rescue and assumed that everyone on the plane was dead. "It was the lowest low I had ever felt," he said later.

Going Back in the Plane?

One woman sitting safely on a raft actually yearned to return to the flooded, sinking Airbus. Emma Cowan, a 26-year-old Australian singer, wanted to retrieve her passport. She was talked out of it by two other passengers.

Cowan later phoned her mother. "Mum, I have been in a plane crash, but I'm still alive," Cowan said. "Why didn't you grab your handbag?" her mother asked.[4]

"I was asking myself, 'What else could I have done?' . . . I felt like I'd been hit by a bus. I had this feeling of shock and disbelief."[5] Only later did a friend tell him that everyone had survived. Harten told Sullenberger that his relief was beyond words.

Treatment of the passengers began in a makeshift triage center aboard a dinner boat. Firefighters wrapped cold passengers with linen tablecloths. Doctors and nurses at hospitals that received the passengers were pleasantly surprised so few were hurt. St. Luke's-Roosevelt Hospital Center treated ten patients, mostly for hypothermia. Flight attendant Doreen Welsh was treated for a lacerated leg.

Sullenberger tried to confirm the number of survivors. He did not learn that all 155 on the plane had pulled through until several hours later. That knowledge brought him tremendous comfort. "I remember

One Crash—Then Another

US Airways experienced two crashes on January 15, 2009. The first was the crash landing of Flight 1549. The second was the crash of its Web site due to high traffic.

In the first hour after the descent into the Hudson River, the Web site was slow to load and viewers could not find out the status of the flight and passengers. Soon the entire Web page was down. US Airways finally opened a new page dedicated to updating viewers on the landing and rescue.

feeling the most intense feeling of relief that I ever felt in my life," he said. "I felt like the whole weight of the universe had been lifted off my heart."[6]

Everyone aboard Flight 1549 was deeply affected by the trauma they had experienced. Their lives had changed forever. They had become heroes. And nobody was embraced as a greater hero than Sullenberger. ⌒

After all passengers had been evacuated, the US Airways jet rested in the frigid Hudson River.

*Passenger Clay Presley hugged his daughter
after returning home to Charlotte.*

NO RETURN TO NORMAL

The near-death experience changed everyone on board Flight 1549 in a profound way. Most returned to their same lifestyles, but would remain affected mentally and emotionally by the experience.

For many, the changes were immediate. Bill Elkin became overwhelmed by emotion the first time he was alone after the incident. He cried for 45 minutes in his hotel room as he recalled the terror he felt during the descent over the Hudson. He later suffered through periods of depression and loneliness.

Survivors expressed a greater zest for life and deeper appreciation for family members and friends. Moments with loved ones they once considered insignificant now took on more meaning and provided more joy. Irina Levshina learned to show her positive feelings for others more easily. "In all kinds of relationships with people, if you want to express something, your appreciation, your love, you shouldn't delay those things," she said. "Just do them."[1]

Jennifer Doyle was positively affected by the selfless attitude of fellow passengers, as well as the

Flying Again

Some passengers aboard Flight 1549 have avoided flying ever since the bird strike brought their plane down. Others resumed flying right away because they did not want to give in to their fears.

Don Norton took the latter approach. He was in a plane bound for Los Angeles a few days later to appear on *The Ellen DeGeneres Show*. He was also soon flying to Connecticut for a surprise party for his brother. Before he left for that trip, he posted a message on Facebook that read, "Watch out, geese, here I come!"[2]

rescuers. That gave her a brighter outlook about people in general. "It's a healthy reminder that people are good and people do look after each other and care about each other," she said.[3]

Some aboard Flight 1549 became instant celebrities, if only for a few days. They were hounded for media interviews to describe the horror they had endured and the relief they now felt. Several were guests on such national talk shows as *Late Night with David Letterman* and *The Ellen DeGeneres Show*.

Finally Going Golfing

Several passengers on Flight 1549 were friends heading to a golfing vacation in Myrtle Beach, South Carolina. The trip was canceled after the plane went down. The golfing buddies rescheduled the excursion for three months later. On that occasion, however, they refrained from stepping onto another airplane. They drove to the site instead.

BIG DAY IN THE BIG APPLE

A feeling of relief swept New York. What could have been a tragedy that rekindled memories of the 2001 terrorist attacks, was instead described by some as a miracle. Among those who used that term was New York Governor David A. Paterson, who praised Sullenberger and those who contributed to the rescue efforts. He said,

We've had a miracle on the Hudson. This pilot, somehow, without any engines, was somehow able to land this plane. This is a potential tragedy that may have become one of the most magnificent days in the history of New York City agencies.[4]

Sullenberger later admitted that he had a difficult time sleeping in the nights that followed. He was tormented by the thought that he could have done something better. He finally reached the point at which he felt no regrets.

The most touching moment in the days that followed was a reunion between the Flight 1549

New Gig for "Sully"

Americans became accustomed to seeing Sullenberger on television after he safely landed Flight 1549. His popularity and knowledge motivated TV network CBS to hire him in May 2011 as an on-air aviation expert.

Sullenberger debuted by speaking with news anchor Harry Smith about the crash of an Air France flight into the Atlantic Ocean in 2009. Seventy-five bodies were pulled out of the water during the week before the interview.

Though he retired from piloting in 2010, Sullenberger remained concerned with problems in the aviation industry. "We can't assume that because aviation has continued to get safer—accidents are relatively rare now—that we're doing everything right," he said. "We have to keep actively looking for continuous improvements."[5]

Among the chief problems at the time Sullenberger retired were reports of air traffic controllers falling asleep on the job. He claimed that if work schedules of controllers, pilots, mechanics, and flight attendants did not allow for more sleep time, "then ultimately we're going to create situations where the system will fail."[6]

passengers and crew in Charlotte. The event was organized by *60 Minutes*, the news documentary program. Sullenberger was moved by the gratitude expressed by those whose lives he saved.

"More than one woman came up to me and said thank you for not making me a widow," he said. "[There were men who said] thank you for letting my three-year-old son have a father."[7]

They were not the only people giving thanks. Sullenberger emerged as an international hero. He was invited to receive recognition at the Super Bowl and the inauguration ball for newly elected President Barack Obama. His hometown of Danville, California, hosted an event in his honor attended by 2,000 residents. He received letters from admirers around the world.

Chatting with the President

Sullenberger had a humorous conversation with President Barack Obama that included their wives in a private meeting during the 2009 inauguration ball.

Obama asked Lorrie Sullenberger if the fame Chesley had received had gone to his head. She replied that though he had become a hero, he still snored. First Lady Michelle Obama chimed in that the president also snores.

Sullenberger and Skiles have used their newfound fame to speak out on behalf of pilot and flight safety concerns.

Using Fame to Help Others

Sullenberger soon decided that his fame and experience could be used as an advocate for aviation safety. He retired from piloting at the age of 59 in March 2010, and he turned his focus to promoting the piloting profession to younger generations. He had grown concerned that changes in the industry were deterring young people from becoming pilots. As he told a reporter at the time,

There is so much pressure to hire people with less experience. Their salaries are so low that people with greater experience will not take those jobs. We have some carriers that have hired pilots with only a few hundred hours of experience. . . . There's simply no substitute for experience in terms of aviation safety.[8]

Tying the Knot with a Special Guest

Andrew Gray and Stephanie King expressed their love for each other as the Airbus descended into the Hudson River. The engaged couple assumed they were going to die together.

They were thrilled to be wrong. Gray and King married in Wisconsin five months later. Among the invited guests at their wedding was Skiles.

Skiles became vice president of the Coalition of Airline Pilots Association and devoted himself to advocating for pilot and flight safety issues. A year after the landing, he reflected on how the experience motivated him to speak out. "Right or wrong," he said, "we have become the voice of airline pilots. I thought it was my responsibility to take that up and embrace that role."[9]

Skiles and Sullenberger became chairmen of the Experimental Aircraft Association Young Eagles program. The program takes children up in small planes to further their interest in aviation.

Sullenberger hopes the pilots of tomorrow never experience what he did on January 15, 2009. Despite his early self-doubt following that fateful afternoon, he gained great pride in his achievement. Sullenberger did not merely save the lives of 154 others. He saved the lives of all of their descendants yet unborn.

His wife, Lorrie, shed tears as she read a letter to her husband from the son of an 84-year-old man named Herman Bomze. Bomze was a survivor of the Holocaust, the systematic murder of 6 million Jews by the Nazis during World War II (1939–1945). The elder Bomze watched the drama of Flight 1549 unfold from his apartment window. The letter read:

> *Had you not been so skilled, my father or others like him in their sky-high buildings could have perished along with your passengers had you not landed in the river as you had. As a Holocaust survivor, my father taught me that to save a life is to save a world as you never know what the person you save nor his or her prodigy will go on to contribute to the peace and healing of the world.*[10]

Sullenberger said he was more touched by that note than any other. In his return letter to the son of the Holocaust survivor, Sullenberger wrote, "As I will live on in your life, you will live on in mine."[11]

At least 155 people have lived on because of Chesley Sullenberger and Jeffrey Skiles. ⌐

Sullenberger and Skiles attended a celebration of the one-year anniversary of their successful emergency landing.

TIMELINE

January 15, 2009 3:03 p.m.	3:24.54
Flight 1549 leaves the gate at LaGuardia Airport.	The plane is cleared for takeoff from Runway 4.

3:27:36	3:27.42	3:27.49
Pilot Chesley Sullenberger reports that the plane has hit birds and that it is heading back to LaGuardia.	Air traffic controller Patrick Harten confirms a return to LaGuardia and orders the plane to turn left at 220 degrees.	Harten stops all departures from LaGuardia to make room for Flight 1549.

3:25.51

Pilot Jeffrey Skiles informs the air traffic controller that the plane is at 700 feet (213 m) and climbing.

3:27.01

Radar shows the plane intersect with what turns out to be a flock of geese while rising between 2,900 and 3,000 feet (884 and 914 m).

3:28.05

Harten asks Sullenberger if he would prefer to land on Runway 13.

3:28.11

Sullenberger tells Harten he will be unable to land at LaGuardia and might be forced to bring the plane down in the Hudson River.

3:28.31

Harten reiterates his offer to direct the plane to LaGuardia, but is rejected again by Sullenberger.

TIMELINE

3:28.50	3:28.55	3:29.03
Sullenberger asks Harten about the availability at Teterboro Airport in New Jersey.	Harten confirms opening at Teterboro.	Sullenberger agrees to land at Teterboro.

3:31	3:31	3:32
The plane touches down in the water. Most of the plane remains intact as the passengers hurriedly begin evacuating.	Commuter ferryboats and other watercraft begin to converge on the Airbus.	New York Police Department officers board a boat in the Hudson River to begin its rescue operations.

3:29.21

3:29.25

3:29.28

Harten informs
Sullenberger of
availability of
Runway 1 at
Teterboro.

Sullenberger decides
a landing at Teterboro
is too risky. He
tells Harten that he
cannot land there.

Sullenberger confirms
his intention to land
the Airbus in the river.

3:36

4:20

The New York
Fire Department
sends a rescue boat
to the scene.

Sullenberger reports
to the fire department
that everyone is
off the plane.

ESSENTIAL FACTS

DATE OF EVENT

January 15, 2009

PLACE OF EVENT

- ❖ LaGuardia Airport
- ❖ The sky above the airport and the Hudson River
- ❖ Hudson River

KEY PLAYERS

- ❖ Captain Chesley Sullenberger
- ❖ First Officer Jeffrey Skiles
- ❖ Air traffic controller Patrick Harten
- ❖ Flight attendants Donna Dent and Doreen Welsh
- ❖ 150 passengers

HIGHLIGHTS OF EVENT

❖ US Airways Flight 1549 collides with a group of Canada geese shortly after takeoff from LaGuardia Airport.

❖ Pilots Chesley Sullenberger and Jeffrey Skiles conduct an emergency landing in the Hudson River.

❖ New York City emergency personnel and local rescue crews work quickly to ensure that all 155 passengers and flight crew of Flight 1549 survive the crash landing.

QUOTE

"I had accepted death. But then I just got this gift. I think it was Divine Intervention. I went absolutely insane and started pushing people out, telling them to get on the wings."—*flight attendant Doreen Welsh*

GLOSSARY

air traffic controller
> The person who directs planes into and out of airport runways.

airline
> A company that owns and operates planes, usually for the business of transporting passengers.

bird strike
> The collision between birds and an airplane, generally in the air.

flight attendant
> An airline employee who tends to the safety of passengers on a plane.

gliding
> The skill of flying a plane that is not under engine power.

inbound
> Inward bound.

life preserver
> A thick, buoyant jacket that allows people to stay afloat in the water.

Quick Reference Handbook
> A reference guide used by pilots to direct step-by-step action in the event of an emergency.

runway
> Long, usually paved strips on airport property on which planes take off and land.

thrust
> The force used by an engine to propel a plane forward.

ADDITIONAL RESOURCES

SELECTED BIBLIOGRAPHY

Firman, Dorothy, and Quirk, Kevin. *Brace for Impact*. Deerfield Beach, FL: Health Communications, 2009. Print.

Langewiesche, William. *Fly By Wire: The Geese, The Glide, The Miracle on the Hudson*. New York: Farrar, Straus and Giroux, 2009. Print.

Pickert, Kate, and Altman, Alex. "Plane in the Water: How Flight 1549 Averted Tragedy." *Time* magazine. 15 Jan. 2009. Web.

Prochnau, William, and Parker, Laura. *Miracle on the Hudson: The Survivors of Flight 1549*. New York: Ballantine, 2009. Print.

Sullenberger, Chesley, with Zaslow, Jeffrey. *Highest Duty: My Search for What Really Matters*. New York: William Morrow, 2009. Print.

FURTHER READINGS

Atkins, Jeannine. *Wings and Rockets: The Story of Women in Air and Space*. New York: Farrar, Straus and Giroux, 2003. Print.

Grant, R.G. *Flight: 100 Years of Aviation*. New York: DK, 2007. Print.

Morris, Deborah. *Plane Crash and Other True Stories*. Farmington Hills, MI: Thorndike, 2004. Print.

Rowell, Rebecca. *Charles Lindbergh: Groundbreaking Aviator*. Edina, MN: ABDO, 2010. Print.

Web Links

To learn more about the Hudson plane landing, visit ABDO Publishing Company online at **www.abdopublishing.com**. Web sites about the Hudson plane landing are featured on our Book Links page. These links are routinely monitored and updated to provide the most current information available.

Places to Visit

Cradle of Aviation Museum
One Davis Avenue, Garden City, NY 11530
516-572-4111
http://www.cradleofaviation.org/
Visitors can see 75 different air- and spacecraft in eight separate exhibit galleries in this museum. Other features include the Long Island Air and Space Museum and the Giant Screen Dome Theater.

LaGuardia Airport
The Port Authority of New York and New Jersey,
Flushing, NY 11371
718-533-3400
http://www.panynj.gov/airports/laguardia.html
Visitors can watch arrivals and departures and see all the activity surrounding one of the busiest airports in the United States.

The Museum of Flight
9404 East Marginal Way S., Seattle, WA 98108-4097
http://www.museumofflight.org/
More than 150 permanent historic air- and spacecraft exhibits and collections are featured in this museum.

Source Notes

Chapter 1. Just Another Day?

1. William Langewiesche. *Fly By Wire: The Geese, The Glide, The Miracle on the Hudson*. New York: Farrar, Straus and Giroux, 2009. Print. 13.

2. Abbie Boudreau and Scott Zamost. "Passengers report scare on earlier US Airways Flight 1549." *CNN*. CNN, 19 Jan. 2009. Web. 28 July 2011.

3. William Langewiesche. *Fly By Wire: The Geese, The Glide, The Miracle on the Hudson*. New York: Farrar, Straus and Giroux, 2009. Print. 46.

Chapter 2. The Molding of a Pilot

1. Chesley Sullenberger with Jeffrey Zaslow. *Highest Duty: My Search for What Really Matters*. New York: William Morrow, 2009. Print. 3.

2. Ibid. 5–7.

3. Ibid. 19.

4. William Langewiesche. *Fly By Wire: The Geese, The Glide, The Miracle on the Hudson.* New York: Farrar, Straus and Giroux, 2009. Print. 11.

Chapter 3. Winged, Flying Pests

1. Glenn Collins. "With Eye on Airports, City to Begin Culling Geese." *New York Times.* New York Times, 12 June 2009. Web. 28 July 2011.

2. LiveScience Staff. "Migratory Geese Downed Flight 1549 in Hudson River." *LiveScience.* TechMediaNetwork.com, 8 June 2009. Web. 28 July 2011.

3. William Prochnau and Laura Parker. *Miracle on the Hudson: The Survivors of Flight 1549.* New York: Ballantine, 2009. Print. 26.

4. William Langewiesche. *Fly By Wire: The Geese, The Glide, The Miracle on the Hudson.* New York: Farrar, Straus and Giroux, 2009. Print. 49.

Chapter 4. The Collision

1. William Prochnau and Laura Parker. *Miracle on the Hudson: The Survivors of Flight 1549.* New York: Ballantine, 2009. Print. 29.

2. Ibid. 37.

3. "US Air 1549 crash survivor Darren Beck CNN Larry King Live 11FEB2009." *YouTube.* YouTube, 12 Feb. 2009. Web. 28 July 2011.

4. Chesley Sullenberger with Jeffrey Zaslow. *Highest Duty: My Search for What Really Matters.* New York: William Morrow, 2009. Print. 207.

5. William Prochnau and Laura Parker. *Miracle on the Hudson: The Survivors of Flight 1549.* New York: Ballantine, 2009. Print. 39.

Chapter 5. Calm on the Outside, Panic on the Inside

1. Dorothy Firman and Kevin Quirk. *Brace for Impact.* Deerfield Beach, FL: Health Communications, 2009. Print. 74.

2. William Prochnau and Laura Parker. *Miracle on the Hudson: The Survivors of Flight 1549.* New York: Ballantine, 2009. Print. 42.

3. Ibid. 40-41.

4. Chesley Sullenberger with Jeffrey Zaslow. *Highest Duty: My Search for What Really Matters.* New York: William Morrow, 2009. Print. 211.

5. William Langewiesche. *Fly By Wire: The Geese, The Glide, The Miracle on the Hudson.* New York: Farrar, Straus and Giroux, 2009. Print. 75.

6. "Ellen Interviews Passengers from U.S. Airways Flight 1549! – The Ellen DeGeneres Show." *YouTube.* YouTube, 22 Jan. 2009. Web. 28 July 2011.

7. Jeff Wilkins, Christina Boyle, Lisa Lucas, and Greg Lacour. "Surprise Gift to Gal Makes B-day Splash." *NYDailyNews.com.* NYDailyNews.com, 17 Jan. 2009. Web. 28 July 2011.

8. William Prochnau and Laura Parker. *Miracle on the Hudson: The Survivors of Flight 1549.* New York: Ballantine, 2009. Print. 54.

Chapter 6. "Brace for Impact!"

1. "Hudson River Crash Documentary - *The Miracle on Hudson River* - US Airways 1549 – Part 2." *YouTube.* YouTube, 13 Mar. 2009. Web. 28 July 2011.

2. Chesley Sullenberger with Jeffrey Zaslow. *Highest Duty: My Search for What Really Matters.* New York: William Morrow, 2009. Print. 230.

3. William Prochnau and Laura Parker. *Miracle on the Hudson: The Survivors of Flight 1549.* New York: Ballantine, 2009. Print. 52.

4. Dorothy Firman and Kevin Quirk. *Brace for Impact.* Deerfield Beach, FL: Health Communications, 2009. Print. 58.

5. Chesley Sullenberger with Jeffrey Zaslow. *Highest Duty: My Search for What Really Matters.* New York: HarperCollins, 2009. Print. 287.

6. Frances Fiorino. "Update – Flight 1549 Inside the Cockpit, Inside the Cabin." *Aviation Week.* The McGraw-Hill Companies, 17 Jan. 2009. Web. 28 July 2011.

Source Notes Continued

7. William Prochnau and Laura Parker. *Miracle on the Hudson: The Survivors of Flight 1549.* New York: Ballantine, 2009. Print. 59.

8. Ibid. 225.

Chapter 7. The Crash

1. William Prochnau and Laura Parker. *Miracle on the Hudson: The Survivors of Flight 1549.* New York: Ballantine, 2009. Print. 72, 76.

2. Chesley Sullenberger with Jeffrey Zaslow. *Highest Duty: My Search for What Really Matters.* New York: William Morrow, 2009. Print. 239.

3. William Prochnau and Laura Parker. *Miracle on the Hudson: The Survivors of Flight 1549.* New York: Ballantine, 2009. Print. 91.

4. William Langewiesche. *Fly By Wire: The Geese, The Glide, The Miracle on the Hudson.* New York: Farrar, Straus and Giroux, 2009. Print. 9-10.

5. Rick Newman. "How Sullenberger Really Saved US Airways Flight 1549." *usnews.com.* U.S. News and World Report, 3 Feb. 2009. Web. 28 July 2011.

6. William Prochnau and Laura Parker. *Miracle on the Hudson: The Survivors of Flight 1549.* New York: Ballantine, 2009. Print. 95.

Chapter 8. Trying to Stay Alive

1. William Prochnau and Laura Parker. *Miracle on the Hudson: The Survivors of Flight 1549.* New York: Ballantine, 2009. Print. 97.

2. Ibid. 138.

3. Kate Pickert and Alex Altman. "Plane in the Water: How Flight 1549 Averted Tragedy." *Time.* Time Inc., 15 Jan. 2009. Web. 28 July 2011.

4. William Prochnau and Laura Parker. *Miracle on the Hudson: The Survivors of Flight 1549.* New York: Ballantine, 2009. Print. 104.

5. Dorothy Firman and Kevin Quirk. *Brace for Impact.* Deerfield Beach, FL: Health Communications, 2009. Print. 109.

6. William Prochnau and Laura Parker. *Miracle on the Hudson: The Survivors of Flight 1549.* New York: Ballantine, 2009. Print. 115.

Chapter 9. The Rescue

1. Rebecca Spitz. "Waterway Rescuers Remember Effort To Save Flight 1549." *NY1.com.* NY1 News and Time Warner Cable Inc., 14 Jan. 2010. Web. 28 July 2011.

2. Chesley Sullenberger with Jeffrey Zaslow. *Highest Duty: My Search for What Really Matters.* New York: William Morrow, 2009. Print. 246.

3. Dennis Murphy. "'Brace Yourself for Impact.'" *msnbc.com.* msnbc.com, 17 Jan. 2009. Web. 28 July 2011.

4. Holly Byrnes and Stuart McLean. "Australian Survivor Emma Cowan Tells of Calm before Plane Crashed into New York's Hudson River." *Adelaide Now.* News Limited, 16 Jan. 2009. Web. 28 July 2011.

5. Chesley Sullenberger with Jeffrey Zaslow. *Highest Duty: My Search for What Really Matters.* New York: William Morrow, 2009. Print. 252.

6. "Part 4 of Sully on 60 Minutes." *YouTube.* YouTube, 9 Feb. 2009. Web. 28 July 2011.

Chapter 10. No Return to Normal

1. William Prochnau and Laura Parker. *Miracle on the Hudson: The Survivors of Flight 1549.* New York: Ballantine, 2009. Print. 226.

2. Dorothy Firman and Kevin Quirk. *Brace for Impact.* Deerfield Beach, FL: Health Communications, 2009. Print. 137.

3. William Prochnau and Laura Parker. *Miracle on the Hudson: The Survivors of Flight 1549.* New York: Ballantine, 2009. Print. 220.

4. Robert D. McFadden. "Pilot Is Hailed After Jetliner's Icy Plunge." *NYTimes.com.* The New York Times Company, 16 Jan. 2009. Web. 28 July 2011.

5. David Bauder. "Hero pilot is ready for new CBS News job." *Yahoo! News.* The Associated Press, 1 June 2011. Web. 28 July 2011.

6. Ibid.

7. "Part 5 of Sully on 60 Minutes." *YouTube.* YouTube, 9 Feb. 2009. Web. 28 July 2011.

8. Vivian Nereim. "Flight attendant involved in Hudson crash retires after four decades." *Pittsburgh Post-Gazette.* PG Publishing Co., Inc., 4 Mar. 2010. Web. 28 July 2011.

9. Alan Levin. "Pilots Recall 'Miracle on the Hudson' one year later." *USATODAY.com.* USA TODAY, 14 Jan. 2010. Web. 28 July 2011.

10. "Part 5 of Sully on 60 Minutes." YouTube, 9 Feb. 2009. Web. 28 July 2011.

11. Chesley Sullenberger with Jeffrey Zaslow. *Highest Duty: My Search for What Really Matters.* New York: William Morrow, 2009. Print. 287.

INDEX

ABOUT THE AUTHOR

Martin Gitlin is a freelance writer based in Cleveland, Ohio. He has written more than 40 educational books. Gitlin has won more than 45 awards during his 25 years as a writer, including first place for general excellence from the Associated Press.

PHOTO CREDITS

Steven Day/AP Images, cover, 3, 68, 72; Seth Wenig/AP Images, 6; Mark Lennihan/AP Images, 11, 96 (top); Amriphoto/iStockphoto, 13; Mike Kaplan/U.S. Air Force Photo, 14; USAF Academy/AP Images, 19; Bebeto Matthews/AP Images, 23, 76; Josh Reynolds/ AP Images, 24; Michael Stubblefield/iStockphoto, 28; Little Rock (Ark.) National Airport/AP Images, 31; John Tlumacki/AP Images, 33; Peter ten Broecke/iStockphoto, 34; Klaas Lingbeek-van Kranen/iStockphoto, 39; Trela Media/AP Images, 41, 98 (top); Red Line Editorial, 42, 48, 97; Susan Walsh/AP Images, 51; Andrew Theodorakis/New York Daily News Archive/Getty Images, 52; Henny Ray Abrams/AP Images, 56, 96 (bottom); Gary O'Brien/The Charlotte Observer/AP Images, 59, 86; Terry Singh/ Getty Images, 60; New York City office of the Mayor/AP Images, 63, 98 (bottom); Neilson Barnard/Getty Images, 67; Alexandre Valerio/AP Images, 75; Mario Tama/Getty Images, 81, 99; Frank Franklin II/AP Images, 85; Mark Wilson/Getty Images, 91; David Goldman/AP Images, 95